William Wall

Fahrenheit Says Nothing To Me

DEDALUS

The Dedalus Press
24 The Heath ~ Cypress Downs ~ Dublin 6W
Ireland

© William Wall and The Dedalus Press 2004

ISBN 1 904556 21 3 paper
ISBN 1 904556 22 1 bound

"The Wasp's Nest" won the American Ireland Fund/Writers' Week Award. "Q" was published in the Autumn 2003 edition of The SHOp. Many thanks to John and Hilary Wakeman for suggestions about the structure.

Dante "Inferno Canto V" various stanzas first published in *The Irish Times*

The Dedalus Press is represented and distributed in the U.S.A. and Canada by **Dufour Editions Ltd.**, P.O. Box 7, Chester Springs, Pennsylvania 19425
in the UK by **Central Books**, 99 Wallis Road, London E9 5LN

The Dedalus Press receives financial assistance from
An Chomhairle Ealaíon, The Arts Council,
Ireland.
Printed in Dublin by Johnswood Press

FAHRENHEIT SAYS NOTHING TO ME

WILLIAM WALL

THE DEDALUS PRESS

Contents

Winter's Wasps	9
Aerial Bombardment	11
The Butcher	12
The Old Rise from the Dead Trick	13
The Death of Insects	14
On Surfaces	15
On Dwelling in Silence	16
Encounters with Whales	17
I'm Afraid of America	20
Fahrenheit Says Nothing To Me	21
Postcards from The Inferno	23
Meditations with Coleridge	26
After Horace III.1	29
The Land of the Troglodytes	31
On the Character of the Light	34
The Stairs Unlit	35
Light	36
The Wasp's Nest	37
Inscriptions	40
Alice falling	43
Going to Bed with the Snowman	44
Winter Holiday	45
Birthday at Moulin de Mohots	46
The Stone Anchor	47
Rooms	48
Prayer for Riding in Front	49
Emergency Surgery: Brain Tumour	50
Q	52
Five Dreams	64

Who Made the World	66
Catechism	67
Mirror	68
The Old Venetian Lighthouse on Cephalonia	69
The Frame-Maker's Workshop	70
The Coming of Fire to Ireland	71
The Practice of Listening to Shells	72
Winter Diary	73
The Shield-Maker	79
The Body of a Young Fisherman	80
Alfred Russell Wallace in the Molluccas	81
Some Observations on the Origin of the Species	82

for Liz, Illan and Oisín

Winter's Wasps

Winter's wasps emerge
to a changed world
and nothing in their code
prepares them.

No one more dedicated
to reputation
they wave their tails
like affidavits

But days dishearten
restless nights
hushed by frost
a difficult dawn.

Children desert
their summer fruit
the vitreous sun
sucks icicles.

There is no enemy
manifest
no-one bares arms
no summer larks.

Pretence has served us well
our yellow and black
battle-standards
advertising pain.

Now a lien on our days
our flight sequestered
we fold our faultless wings
and curse celebrity.

Aerial Bombardment

Velcroed to the whitewash
neglect shelters the bats
dead eyes following the conversation.

At night they flit by rafters
shadows coming in on radar
they fill our sleep

the turbulent silence
of their passage
jamming our dreams.

Though they have not touched us
fear complicates the ballistics
and nobody knows what they want.

The Butcher

Lives drift in shambles
shit and blood and flies
the punctuating thud

of the humane killer.
Splay-foot on the tiles
the butcher dreaming cunt

idling over the details
filling out forms
sees himself inside the carnival

the heart of the world.
No one will question
his assessment

his weights and measures
so many sides.
He works on piece-work

every cut a work of art.
No one can touch him here.
Carnage is his daughter.

The Old Rise from the Dead Trick

A wren skulking
among the stooped daffodils
a sly old king.

Hunted up and hunted down
he plans to pull the usual stunt
having survived the revolution.

Easter is a week from now
but I have the measure of him
where he's lying low.

The boys are gathering
the croppy chetniks.
Oh the business end of a pointy stick

and the songs we'll sing.

The Death of Insects

Silent the ant's death
a carcass of needles
and canted pins
jackknives.

Woodlice evacuate.
You look and there's nothing in them
in dark places.
A puff disperses hundreds

light as motes, shells of air.
In their remainder, a narrative
B&W negatives on the Nagasaki wall.
This is the way they go

to the 11th hour
(a line of DDT is the front) the ants
come over for medals
straightening the line

building redoubts
the roman woodlice form up
advance with caution

(never retreat withdraw).
The sally stalls   gas boys gas.
No one believes in masks
on the thin white line.

Once in a lifetime we hear
their tiny latin krake
and afterwards
noise settles in everything.

On Surfaces

I
Nasturtiums in frost
boiled finger-flesh
time in the skeleton
the sediment of cells.

II
And an ammonite
complex fractured formulaic
tilted on a wet slab
the sky gleaming in it.

III
First among equals
the robin redbreast
listening for worms
in the new-cut grass.

IV
Blood from a bloodbath
the breast's red-brown
invincible
behind the counterfeit wound.

On Dwelling in Silence

How many have we lost
to the leaden echo?
We adapt to anguish
in the 6 o'clock news
one man's meat
and another man's poison
the Hallowe'en treat
and the grave grenade.

And then there is silence: remember?
The occasional passing car
seabirds in the mud of the bay
the casual ticking
of a house settling into night
and no one breathing.

Encounters with Whales

for my sister's chernobyl children

I
Space balloons with whale-song
the moaning
the shrieks the whistling.
Certain stars are dead whales
heads popped

by Queequegg's nuclear dart.
Canst thou draw leviathan
with an hook?
The fingerprint of chaos
detected in galactic spirals

surface eddies   upwellings
whale-ghosts
swirling in ether
waiting for us.
They have taken to infinity

like ducks to water.
Time is leviathan
and their presence
is strong enough
to navigate by.

II
The sea is black,
glassdarkened unfathomable.
What is the bottom here?
The chart says sand and shale
the broken skin

of another world
through which the whales
loop into air to look at us.
We see them
by the faint refraction

of sunlight in their blows
and dorsal fins
like periscopes ranging in.
Mizzen Head Fastnet Galley
lights ignite in memory

the noisy alleyways
of the Atlantic and in all this sea
they pass below our keel.
Their phosphor ghosts
stream under us displacing

nothing. We scramble to the side
and see ourselves in their shadow.
When they breach again
they are going away from us
in the middle distance.

III
And the papers say
a country has gone free
the Larsen Ice-Shelf
a glacier easing its stays.
Whales play there

their symphonies
echo-sounding the ceiling
the melting un-firmament.
Barren is the word
in the Southern Ocean

and a hazard to shipping
people will die. *Canst thou draw
leviathan with an hook?*
Elsewhere there is secession
the creaking of winter

ice moving in the heart
grey-faced children
and old men and the dying women
and the surgeon's mask
who can carve a child from tallow.

We warm them
in quilts of ticking dust
the crackle and spit poisoning sleep
all the uneasy first-born
eyes sharp as needle-tips

second-guessing what we will do next.
This is a respectable nation
we own a version of the present.
Still the world is full
of fragments of our undoing.

I'm Afraid of America

Oh the end of history
and other empty phrases
deconstructionism
fol dee fol di
and we're all afraid of America
now.

I'm for the frogs and the krauts
and the koranic library
and other awkward compromises
but I'm afraid of America
now.

No pax americana
son of rule brittannia
and other risible latinisms.
No war on terror
and the old rogue state

but one day the boys
will bring the whole thing down
Kilmichael in the Western Desert
Tom Barry Bin Laden
fol dee fol di
because we're all afraid of America
now.

Fahrenheit Says Nothing To Me
> I am not used to measuring temperature on the Fahrenheit scale.
> Hence such a measure of temperature says nothing to me.
> — Wittgenstein, *Philosophical Investigations* #509

Me too, Ludwig,
and the following also —
the dogs in the street
who know things
say nothing to me

tarot cards
tea-leaves
economists
pictures
give me a thousand words any day.

For certain reasons
I have trouble
with *res ipsa loquitur*
and the sworn testimony
of a superintendent

government press statements
The Irish Independent
the income returns of publicans
the pro-life movement
toilet humour   soccer.

Daddy Bush and Baby Bush
Black Bush and the burning bush
Ronald Reagan and Donald Duck
mind body spirit
and the great American Novel
and American movies

say nothing to me
The queen of England
her heirs and successors
and her so-called court
and Philip Larkin
say nothing to me

Banks insurance companies pension funds
right of way on roundabouts
cats turnips
and Jehovah's Witnesses
do not speak to me.
Women's tights e-books

tongue-rings do not speak
or navel-rings
labia rings
the ring of confidence
and the ring of bright water
and the paedophile ring

Sky News
and the ticker tape at the bottom
the Nike swoosh
and the bent toothbrush
and the Fahrenheit scale
say nothing to me.

Postcards from the Inferno
nessun maggior dolore
che ricordarsi del tempo felice
nella miseria

I
Postcard from the Inferno

A thousand souls
crossed at the ford
dry-shod.

I saw a broad field
within the walls

pitted with graves
lit by burning wells
noisy with death.

Like with like
is buried here.

Oh turn your face
to the broken wave
the smoke is black.

II
Reading the Inferno in the Café Paradiso

Reading in poor light
errors accumulate
I see things that have
only a tenuous presence

and closer to home
I miss the numinous

and when the door opens
I will not know one hand
from the other
but the future will be evident.

This is where they'll bang up
all the heretics and epicures
to keep the lid on us
in the Café Paradiso
with the vegetarians.

III
At the Dragon: Lee Fields 2002

Ice at the dragon's feet
smoke on the river
first light without stars.

We never see the sky
this tenebrous winter

and there you are
as it were
calling for a boat
loath as anyone
who never loved water.
I will not take you.

By other roads
other gates
shalt thou come to shore
not by this crossing

the strand
everyone must cross
naked and weak.

My son
the courteous master says
this land of tears.

At evening
the light is vermilion
defeating sentiment
and sleep will come.

IV
Francesca's Love

Love quickly caught in a kindly heart
love which will not be denied
love conducted us to one death.

V
Dante in Exile

Starlings carried on restless wings through the cold
in companies large and small
driven by chance
null hopes to comfort them not rest not even less pain.

I saw them and asked master who are these coming?
More than a thousand passed
whom love had taken from life.
One said no pain is worse than happiness recalled.

Meditations with Coleridge
in a Time of Corruption

I
Old STC constipated solitary thinks
Seán Citizen's unwillingness to enquire
into himself
is the cause of all our errors
private and national,

his own heart fluttering in ether
inclosed by hers
and there was that vulcanian spider-web net of steel
which he knew and feared
its feather-touch and improbability

so close I feel his sighing
hear him shifting in the springs.
Although the prognosis is different
still the privy wound
is a familiar an old friend.

And our state too insufferable
the great exchanging gifts
the campaign contributions
and the arse-licking
the business end of the res pub.

Show me one decent man
in 20 years says he
begod I'll show you the party ticket
he never got.
Lucky in love you and I

we keep ourselves to ourselves
wondering what would his father say
what would the old man say
so and so out with a rifle in 21 or 2
this or that safe house

did he do it for this?
For this man's Cayman account?
and we enquire into ourselves
in case of error
uncertain.

II
At an open bedroom door
with what thoughts you
would nightly open your own
(an eye fixed kindly on me when I am talking).

The poor man we say
tormented and weak
love undid him perhaps.

You could go down for worse
the things he said and did not say
quote unquote.

Wait 'til the papers
get their hands on him
not to mention the taxing master
of the high court.

It may be that we become
in the perfecting of self-awareness
our own nightmare.
Old STC dreamed

the spectrum of a fish's back-bone
which by stretching
and curving itself
became a scorpion.

After Horace III. 1

I fear the venal cliques
and keep my mouth shut —
new things, only lately learned,
for children and fools.

A president for all his power
falls to the gods in time:
they tramp the battlefield;
men drop when they frown.

This man buys land
and conceals his boundaries;
this one is elected;
another is spoken of with care;

the demagogue, the barrister,
the great, the small:
necessity rules all of them;
from the spacious clay.

The politician at the public feast
stares at the carving-knife
in dread; the songs
disturb his peace of mind.

But sleep need not be bought.
Farmer and factory man,
hilltop home and Council estate
all feel its gentling hand.

If the sea is troubled,
or the western wind brings rain,
or stones hail on the vines,
or crops and profits fail,

still be content:
you will not hear the olive trees
complaining of the rain
or the cold stars or the sun.

But the fish feels
the ocean shrinking
when he brushes the breakwater
that the contractor filled with waste,

and fear leaps from the wave
and snatches down the man
from the ship's wheel and the car,
the hired-man on the mole

and the owner. If granite cannot
protect them, why build a fine house
with impressive gates
like all the rest of them?

The Land of the Troglodytes

I
Somewhere the trees turn to stone.
Where does it begin?
Impossible now to tell.
The road ghosting through memory
you travel too quickly in your own slow air
thinking of the immutability
of automobiles.
Only the miles change.

And where there were whitethorn hedges
there are dry-stone walls
instead of gradual hills
the wounded crust of the world thrust up into air
gleaming in the evening.
Our lives go by in the wink
of an eye and everything we do
is inclined to acceleration.

Once upon a time every instant
had its focal clarity
and that was childhood.
Growing older means
living faster, every experience
smeared shapeless edgeless morphic.
Lost lost lost
too much is lost

II
Count the things you forgot to pack:
Lourdes water
gift of a neighbour not of your persuasion;

photos of parents
no one explained when they left
there was nothing between you and eternity;

the household gods who failed the household
they carry the same ballast of guilt
to steady and sink —

gods of doorway and hearth
the spirits of the table
and the bed

(where were you);
address book
for friends whose numbers too have been lost.

III
Stones contrive the bog
reticent perplexing.
Everything is transfigured.
You are hurtling

through the land of the troglodytes
and there is no going back.
Full in the windscreen
Balor's good eye winking.

The sea is infinity.
You are over the edge
of the world.
Look down into space.

How many million stars
can you fall through?
You never look back
in case

stone will defeat your soul.
Stay here
longing for home
how much they

loved you
on a perpetual holiday.
By all means remember
save what you can.

IV
The arrow of time points one way
and one way only.
No cellphone rings

in the past.
You are out of touch
out of sight

out of time out of mind
it's the trip of a lifetime never to be repeated
the perfect escape.

On the Character of the Light

Your hands were small
snowdrops on the dark quilt.
I noticed important changes.
You were less

like your photographs
than you used to be
the centres of your eyes
were whitening

losing the light
like salt-greyed windows.
A time would come
when you would not see me

and I would not know you.
There is no preparing
for the day
it's there before you know

before you see it's gone.
One day at the cusp
of seeing and knowing
the character of the light

your hand in mine
on the sloe-rich satin
like a stranger
handing you from a car.

The Stairs Unlit

I stumble from a dream
in too many rooms
and stop
finding the stairs unlit.

These years later
I must find
the necessary light
descending into darkness

where I found her
as she had been for hours
staring at the rain.
When all the ways are dark

we see at the edge
the edge of things
the city shrouded
in dust and smoke

and the dead come
young men and girls
the bride and bridegroom
our ghosts.

Light
      after Solas, *Seán Ó Ríordáin*

Darkness came
stripe by stripe

until things were extinguished.
Night made black of white.

Chairs became shades.
The room declined

and shadow swallowed everything.
The belly of night is empty

I can feel it under my hand
only loss has the power

to reconstitute the past.
A light and at once

a room emerges
the chairs are restored

my fingers come from nowhere
to carry shape to the world.

When I go out eventually
I will leave the world to itself

but like everyone else
I will leave in the dark.

The Wasp's Nest

Ho paura someone said
and I fear greatly
on a dark night
when the wind is a fiddle-bridge

sounding the body
(your cheek resting on that certain curve
with nonchalance).
My father was a self-taught man

he held the fiddle loosely
like a girl in a reel
uncertain of the next note
and he was afraid as the strokes

ate out his brain.
Remember the wasp-nest
that grew under the rafters
the beauty of the hanging shape

a chinese lantern.
He bore it before him on a hayfork
humming
but it cast no light.

I was charged with opening doors
looking inside and out.
I saw the way he held his head high
tilted like a robin's

but I could not foresee
the fuses going one by one
until the house was dark.
It's true what they say

winter and the small hours
take the older ones
there is always some funeral or other, yes
and the death of fathers is common.

Look out for the early crocus
he used to say
new lambs like paper bags
scattered in the grass

soul-rags on a barbed-wire fence
for death cometh soon or late
the keeper of secrets
scrambling among trinkets

immortal stories.
He could throw nothing out
but the salvage of small things
did not protect him.

Lovers are specialists
trawling for hope
as my father did
as my mother did.

Remember how they would swing away
waltzing on eggshells
his hand on her waist
the happy dancers

conducting their own silence
through the crowded night
the thunderous sky?
(What I am afraid of

is that it is not empty.)
The wind goes down to a bass-viol
in an empty warehouse.
Where are the stars?

We learn that birds sing
long before dawn
and rain in the doorway is soft.
An old wrinkled potato is the soul

growing up with death
and there is toxin there
(they got their teeth in us alright).
So considering the evidence

there is no escape
unless it be you and me
stretched out like spoons in a drawer
sheltering each other.

Inscriptions

I

i.m. Peter Ayles

I hear Elgar's full gale on the cd
the cello driving down my heart.
Elsewhere a door closes.

Liz is saying goodnight to the children
leaving the lights on
and I am listening to the grace-notes

of desolation.
Snow is falling in Italy
and on the stones in Bembridge

where your name is
with the dead divided by winter.
Snow pales on your darkness

poplars and beeches are your pickets.
In your last nightmare
the Dorniers of Alamein returned

Bombers! you cried
or was it the morphine talking?
But last night American bombers stopped here

skaldcrows stooped on the wet tarmac.
Tonight they are falling on your desert
three thousand miles away.

II
>   *i.m. Seán Dunne*

He was looking for god
and certainly he found his place.
He called frequently
to a silence that seemed to betoken.

Now he knows where he is
and whether there was anything
in tenebræ
in the first place.

> The island
> the chapel
> the bolt-holes in stone
> where they knelt down.

He thought the sky's great 0
was o instead of zero
as happens to the best of us
in such places.

III
>
> *for Pete Dobson and Mary Rose O'Neill*
> *i.m. of their son*

Your notebooks record the clutter
the immensity of detail
the bleak laughter of minutiae
each image
a child in its own right
      a two-pin plug
      a shell
      a space ship
      a shoe.

There are things so small
they must be actual.

Everything is shrinking
the scope of the pen
abated
by one child's death.

A clock is unwinding
the subtracted years
as if you could undo his absence
by going backwards.

Alice Falling

Frost is moving on the roof
daylight opening the box
the ticking of morning.

I measure change
in the interval
between the appearance of a drop

and the end of the fall.
Alice is falling
and as she falls she picks things up

she cannot drop them.
Forever is the time
between your sleeping and your waking

before the eyelid opens
I kiss your sleep-softened silence
and we fall together.

Going to Bed with the Snowman

I have gone to bed with the snowman
in the dead of night.
I have seen the lights
gleaming briefly on and off

a radiance that could not
be accounted for
by the humour of the moment
or his perishing crystals.

That nothing is forever
is known and people
live too long these days
but this I can swear

there was a cold kind of loving
when I lived with the snowman.

Winter Holiday

A bad tooth struggles out of a green sea
Baltimore November '97 and I want to tell you
something about water not knowing exactly
what anyone can say about it anymore.
      I want to talk about you

Two boats pair-trawling a mile out lost to the land
the sea swallows their engine noises.
The surge of the wave along the rocks is rapids
a maelstrom see how it liquidates what was rock.
      I want to talk about you

A baby seal-head moons black eyes at us
in the grey line where the spindrift churns off the cliff
wondering where all the mackerel have gone
nets and gins and everything that holds us holds him.
      I want to talk about you

Talk is cheap so sit by me and look out there.
The curve we call the end of the earth is five miles away
if it is the end of the earth I want to hold your hand
and say something about this black rock and green sea.
      I want to talk about you

Birthday at Moulin de Mohots

Thunderous water in the millrace
opening onto the pool
the neon damsel flies
break left and keep low.

Love is a local anguish
but your tongue-tip
brushes mine.
On your hand

nightfall depends
and a low half-moon.
It is always someone's anniversary

in the evening air
but this is our *jour de fête*
after twenty years.

The Stone Anchor

Tenacity is not the only virtue
for ground tackle
and cable is costly.
The stone anchor never fouls

though its holding is not the best.
I never know what will happen next.
When I think of death
I think of cables parting

my mother wanted to die
when my father went
and children die in containers
of asphyxiation

or a frosty welcome
a rough passage.
But the point of departure
is sinister too.

We end where we begin it seems
where we take leave
and who will the pilot be
to sail the hell-ship?

I try not to foresee
imagining the past instead
but all the histories call
this future into existence.

Rooms

There is a room for every tragedy,
the death of children
the death of parents
the fall of an empire,

but I find you in the room of hope
the room of certainty
the room of joy
and the room of rooms

where you sit above a page
a light angled on your right shoulder
your knees folded under you
like some elegant animal,

an eland
or a long-legged big-eyed giraffe
and the actual air expands to accommodate you
and this is also the room of love.

Prayer for Riding in Front

The omens are not good.
Rain overnight
has changed the road
the radio says be careful
confusion is in the way
and the phenomena assemble.
Come back my love
and put your hand on my back
the way you slept last night.

There is no prayer for riding in front
(where presumption goes)
but insurance matters
and an air-bag.
Dawn's rose blooms
under a brushstroke of ash.
Come back my love
and put your hand on my back
the way you slept last night.

Emergency Surgery: Brain Tumour

I
The Bad News

I never pass a day without pain
so long now it has become
the shape of the everyday.
I know a little
of how you feel in that place,

the world's relentless inflation
crowding your head.
What put a thing there
where dreams should be
and what can the knife do?

Is there a blade so clean
it slides between
thought and thing
gliding through the imagination
like a silent-running submarine?

Or what if they weaken the wall
and green sea comes in
a new deluge
everything suspended in perception
like a preserving fluid

when you wake up?

II
Post-op Intensive Care

Although you moved your little finger
although you smiled
better not to wake now.

Although your mother spends her days
asserting your existence
better not to wake now.

Although the only thing that changed
is the world
and you are the same

your face so beautiful
perfect as a child
better not to wake now

better not to wake.

Q

for all the Still's and RA people

Q conspires with God
who appears in a green
gown and wears latex.
He leaves no forensics.

Scalpel, he says.
Q says: Say please.
Clamp, he says.
Say please. Chainsaw.

God is mechanics
and the triumph of engineering
and Q thinks
he is filling up with dead bits.

In the aftermath
he is ecstatic,
drifting between death and sleep
awash with pain.

It's a good one, God says,
a beautiful piece.
Give me a spare rib, he jokes,
and I'll give you a prosthesis.

*

Q forms a secret society.
How will we know? they say.
We all have our secret mark, Q says.
A legless man

a woman with claws
titanium knees
one short leg one long
and a spinal question mark.

We have the worm
in the knuckle
the teredo of bones
and balloon skin.

We are the beautiful,
the heirs,
the aristocracy of pain
and we're in for the long haul.

*

I hate that vulgar crowd,
but I whistle at virgins, he says.
The mighty
auctioneer and valuer,
the client-server,
the politician in his pride,
they go the way of flesh,

but we are immortal
bits and pieces,
non omnis moriar et cetera -
Qdemagogue
Telling it like it is.
Fear enters
by the jugular,

a tidal surge —
regrets and confidences,
I love you
one and all,
but the fish
feels the shrinking
ocean
when he feels the stone.

*

By the absence of evidence,
by a process of elimination,
by all that is good
and all that is warped,
by your leave,
by guess and by god,
by the pricking of thumbs,
by hook or by crook,
by the hokey,
by jaysus,
by the shortcut and long,
by the fields and the road,
by night and by day,
bifurcate and not,
Q knows.

Wake up time Mr Q,
God says, SMILE.

And he did
and glass in the looking-glass broke,
non-shatters shat,
stretchers shrank

and lifts dropped,
and hospital cat
got at the mortuary,
and nurses gave suck
and the world was a worse place
for his waking.

*

He comes to the point.
Pain maketh the man.
(Time flies. His hip is a lace-cap.)
God says, Tried in the fire?
At least I tried.

Q says, I can't take it anymore
and who created Satan
and free will is all my arse.
And God says, Child.
and Q keeps mum,

thinks: Oh all this
is too much,
a bit over the top,
only an infinite mind
could imagine it:

the variety,
the subtlety.
So I believe, said Q
and God went away
laughing.

*

Q is for half-made
self-made half-man
half-man half-hearted
a fine half.

Quasi-fashionable
quasi-made
queasy Q.
Half-a-leg is better

than no-leg,
half a heart follows.
By leaps and by bounds
he travels

always half
the remaining distance,
never actually ending
his half-life

although he has half a mind to,
semi Q demi Q mezzo Q
Q/2
(over one would do).

*

He learned vanishing
in a puff of spores
leaving only his mushroom skin,
the bloat, the steroid moonskin.

People said:
How well you look,
your skin is as fresh.
We expected worse.

Q lingers in the air
like someone's ashes.
Never inhale.
His existence is sinovial.

*

Q is a bat
paragliding corridors,
he beeps and is not heard,
the nightflitter.

His droppings are aluminium,
light white ductile,
they scatter underfoot
like marbles.

He sees everything.
His hearing is above average
even for a bat.
When the treatment stops

he crashes,
a cloud of batspores,
a crumpled tearful child
complaining of pain.

He begs them:
Give me back my bones.
Skin is nothing
but something

to go out in.
I am empty inside,
hollowfibrous Q,
Qpuffball, Qfug.

*

Q's whiskers frisk the brown-eyed nurse.
He sniffs her starch, tickles inner, insinuates.
Things are in there tight and then he is

a slippery brown shape ratting under wear,
tipping at will. She feels him.
'Are we comfy?' she says, taking him in her stride.

*

Q meets The Good Cripple
who smiles at him.
Into each life,

and we all have our cross,
and things could be worse,
and tomorrow is another day.

Q guts him
with a boning knife
and frames his rictus.

In his worst nightmares
those lips come back
to kiss him well,

whispering
Momma's little boy
every child is perfect.

Lies lies,
he screams,
Qed.

*

The surgeon is a graceful man,
his hands are delicate as ice,
he makes the cut,
his pride the micro-zip.

The surgeon is a graceful man,
he has a keen eye
for the beauty
of higher mammals.

Praise the surgeon who slits
who saws the bones
who chisels out the bits
who glues the plastic hip

and leaves
the surreal wires
spinning like electrons
inside.

*

Into the spare room of aspirants,
the transplant hearts, kidneys, livers, eyes,

such delicate valves and bivalves and molluscs,
the plastic hips and knees, *sub specie sterile*.

Q comes in and pokes around, and sneezes.
Naughty naughty Mr Q, sneezing spreads germs.

Haven't you ever heard of handkerchiefs?
God chalks it down to Q, another black one,

a mortaller, because he meant it.
No pleading please, no insanity

in this jurisdiction. What you did
was wrong, naughty naughty Mr Q.

*

I believe in one god, says Q,
who made me what I am.
The bastard knew, he knew,
what I would turn into.

So sue, says god,
I got it covered.
And Q sued
and lost.

*

Q sees that the world
is a point of view
that cannot be upheld,

that everything he can say
has its exact antonym
and if he can assert

both the existence
and the non-existence
of anything

then that thing
is meaningless.
He thinks he is a lost child

in a gingerbread house
eating his way out,
an elderly Alice

gazing at a sepia-tint
of what he was
in the naked long-ago.

*

I Q
being of sound mind
bequeath my body to medicine
until my death

but afterwards
to the brown-eyed nurse
for her particular pleasure
and edification

or as a *memento mori,*
and speaking of which
I leave my mind
donatio mortis causa

to S. Freud and C .G. Jung
to be divided between them
in equal parts
the left side going

to the latter
and the right to the former
and if they predecease me
the whole shooting match

to the cat,
but the dead bits in gratitude
for services rendered
go to God.

*

requiem
Is there anyone in there
when the lights are on
or is it Q
hiding out from the posse?

Come out now
or forever be silent
incubus mine,
my Q.

Your hands will be whole again
risen as you promised,
your legs will be whole again,
your spine will be straight again,

your neck will bend,
and when you come forth
you will have comfort
Q Dante Q phoenix

Lazarus Q.
Here lieth a crook
that was once straight as larch,
claws once piano,

legs marathon,
ramrod spine,
too much neck,
relict of Q

awaiting judgement.
Oh hand me down the judgement
and let there be
in the heel of the hunt

one single day of remission,
and they make the cut
(the flesh is alabaster)
and there for all to see

the last word
QRIP.

Five Dreams

Dream of Flowers
    Who would plant bulbs?
    Shelled mother-of-pearls
    burnt popeyes
    zombie-skins

    they eat the polarity
    of the world
    and then invade the air
    glowing sinister

    amber lights
    in spring gloom
    to enter caveats
    for hasty gardeners.

Dream of Butterflies
    Neat as a swallow
    I am eating butterflies
        a delicacy.
    You warn about violence
    in the opening chrysalis.

Dream of Names
    Broken stones clutter
    the stone-cutter's backyard
        memento mori.
    Death rejected these closures
    none of the spare names are ours.

Dream of Hands
>My hand on the lost
>territory of your arm
>>a sly incursion
>a sally across borders
>infinite delicacy

The Contortionist's Dream
>At the key-parties
>I always draw my own key.
>>They take advantage
>of my flexibility
>with shameful regularity.

Who Made the World

They hang about like corner-boys
fags cupped backwards in palms.
We're looking at the scattering
the glowing tips spread out across
a canopy from the Maglin river
to the top of Carrigrohane.

The world calls it a galaxy
and it has its place
in the theory of everything
but we know it is the lost boys
the angular brylcreemed kings
who warmed the corners of the world
when we were children.

Catechism

In childhood we were told
expect calamity in orchards.
Later we became aware
of the sensuality of apples

and somewhere in between
we adamandeved
and threw ourselves on each other
with conviction in dark doorways,

the first slippery tongue-tip
tasting of silvermints
whispering questions
and unlikely answers.

Cold hands meant a warm heart
in an apple-tight breast
back in the time
of the catechism of flesh.

Mirror

after Specchio, *Salvatore Quasimodo*

Here on the trunk
emeralds emerge
out of the greenheart
the tree's best green
that once seemed dead
doubled over the ditch.

It is the only miracle I know
and I am the clouded water
sharpening a piece of sky
in the canal today
sharpening the trunk's green stone
that until now was wood.

The Old Venetian Lighthouse on Cephalonia

To administer the poverty of Cephalonia
a light in the approach. They built on the faults
that could not be annealed, that moved in 1953.
Enchanted by the lens and what it concealed,
by surfaces, happier on water, they were deceived.

But in the afternoon light we are suspicious of face value.
We test the ground. We know the bend of history
when we see it, the high dry shore,
shivered scarf and tumbled roof, the landlord absentee.
This is our heritage too and we must make the most of it,
the tentative pilotage of living with ourselves.

The Frame-Maker's Workshop
for Con Kelleher, artist and frame-maker

This is where the images go
for definition.
Everything that is beautiful
is in the frame.

The edge of the unknown
is your lathe
the winking blade.
Nothing is wasted.

The eye is the lens
but the heart selects
for each thing
its best-loved place.

The Coming of Fire to Ireland

Water is our element.
The alder and the sally thrive
the whitethorn's cold

glowing on dark skin
the tonguetip
of the blackthorn

the yellowflamed furze.
On sullen summer days
light comes out of another world

and thunder puts its spin
on our drowsy air.
Like everything else

fire came from strangers
(to crack stones
and boil water).

We thought they were gods.
Since then we have not
gone far.

We hunker by the streams
telling elaborate lies
and watching the hillsides burn.

The Practice of Listening to Shells

The sea swivels down
the spirals of a shell
and the ripple lives
in the shell

in the coils of the ear
in air.
Gulls babbling
a bobbing stick

a crab
voices buoyed on the wind
the lost sailor
the lover

the child.
Love dies in sleep
we cannot separate
being there

and being gone.
It slips away.
The border is a breath.
Wave once

and walk away.
Wear clean underwear.

Winter Diary

I
I released a dove
that never came back.

Though the fidelity of doves
is not in doubt
still I think about it

and in the meantime
the weather continues bad.

II
3 weeks of rain
a watery landscape in unsettled light
the tinfoil glitter of seagulls
so far from home.

I came out to clear my head
but the head is the least of my troubles.
I am falling apart
and the world is drowning
only the seagulls escape

into the clear air
carrying a little water
a little earth
to begin again somewhere.

III
Now the world has had enough
of hail and sleet
the river drowns the bridge-arch
and shocks the town.
We who feared terror
fire and famine
now fear water
having seen the river turned
a terrible flood
that drowned the plain.
Here dread succeeds
greater than God
or country
and we have lost our way.

IV
A pigeon hit my window
I saw him on the path
opened a little

like something wooden
struck by a hammer
but not shattered.

He seemed to be thinking things over
considering the flight plan
and where it went wrong

where the sky went
and what conditions
at that height
could create a column of ice.

V
Glass is a supercooled liquid
only rigid on the outside.
Inside
everything is uncertain.

A double-glazed window
contains also
a column of nothing
between the inside outsides

and around the edges
winter
cools in fractals
like a closing lead.

In these erratic currents
I imagine the wreck
of yesterday
and tomorrow

the perfect metaphor
of Endurance
light
over everything.

Hurley's elegant plates
where emptiness
is white
and black is us.

VI
A sun like light on polished steel
and lower down a watery copper
or gold
and the crown of an ashtree

black veins and arteries
drawing virtue down
into the pits.

Countless the dead wait
with upturned faces
for the rain of light.

VII
Tomorrow is the solstice
but tonight is the moon's show.

Making a virtue out of obscurity
she gleams above the mist
like a weak bulb

and the field is blue grey and shapeless.
There are things missing
and things that should not be there.
Midwinter's eve.

I hear a high tide
ticking under the barley stubble
and stones wearing away
and someone leaving
a neighbour's house
in a commotion of casting off and letting go.

VIII
The sun burns through a dying tree
and planes small as motes
swim in the space.
Telegrams of condolence
have been despatched.

After a bad night's work
it is pick-up-the-pieces time.

Chary of loss
weary of love
time and his old tricks
we meet at dawn
for coffee and pistols
but agree on terms instead.

Each move has its own sound
the cracked leaves and ice
lights imploding
on the frozen filaments.
We warm our hands in clouds.

IX
They say there is a cock-step in the evening
everything later today than yesterday
sunset over the barley stubble
and tea.

The decline of winter
is irreversible.
unless there is a war
in which case
everything is here to stay.

Soon there will be lambs
nests
snowdrops
t-shirts
cabbage

showers with sun between
not just showers.
unless there is a war
in which case
everything is here to stay

and the ashtree will be in leaf
latest of them all
and last to fall
the stubborn ordinary

and someone will plough down the stubble
turning the gold over
unless there is a war
in which case
everything is here to stay.

October 2002 - March 2003

The Shield-Maker
on the eve of war 2003

We may say
he made also a great
fallow field

large and three times
over-ploughed already.
Labourers he made there

and ploughboys
turning their horses up and down
furrow by furrow

and the ploughed-land was dark
behind them
though the field was of gold.

The Body of a Young Fisherman
Brought Home in Nets

He comes in with the tide
the young salt
moonpale moonbloated.

His eyes are shells.
In the creeks of his gut
eels swell.

Oh he is lost
and the land
has no pull on him.

He waves
as he arrives
to his last goodbye.

He is the age of the moon
and only his hair
is still twenty nine.

Fishers of men stand
by swings and roundabouts
over the quay

and the dead man looks at us
like a baleful visitor
down on his luck.

Alfred Russell Wallace in the Mollucas

Alfred Russell Wallace in the Molluccas
I know his pain. Night after night
in the light of his specimens
ague and mortification
and the sheer variety of things.
The world is staggering
a sickness itself an infested planet
heedless of reason meaningless hotchpotch.

Then one night the brutal fact
borne in upon him (the fittest survive).
In the meantime there are ulcers
and malaria perhaps gangrene
and all of this to be skinned and shipped
and a letter to Darwin to give the game away.

Some Observations on the Origin of the Species

I
The Evegene
    And after all
    we are all Hottentots —
    I read it in *The Times* —
    can you beat that?

    Old Adam's legacy
    a piece of fancywork
    in the y-chromosome
    a genetic quark.

    Eve too.

    I picture her in genes
    the common ancestor
    a Punch cartoon
    circa nineteen o one.

    and a wet week back
    we were all Martian
    little green bastards
    of a 2 or 3 billion year old
    fuck.

II
Meteor Theory
>A cemetery of whorls
>the empty sepulchres
>of god's big bang
>our name on stone.
>
>A tinkle-less sprinkle
>in the adamant
>a speck in the universal jakes
>the first manmark.

III
On Mendelian Selection
>And old Gregor Mendel teaches us
>that even nature screws up
>(the best laid plans et cetera)
>some sports live
>some sports die
>that's natural
>says Mendel.
>
>The current of generation
>fluctuates once in a while
>hence one piece of shit
>grows legs
>and one remains a piece of shit
>that's natural
>says Mendel.
>
>One walks out of the soup and into air.
>One stillborn
>flops on the rim of water
>evolution's colon or full stop
>that's natural
>says Mendel.

It has nothing to do with desert
else who should scape flogging.
I give thanks that all the infinities
conspired to give me legs.

IV

Pete Dobson's Drawing of a Piece of Clay

A bodiless snout of clay
rests on the wheel
a missing aardvark
a cartoon joke
bad luck old sport.

In each nostril
shadows grow
if this is a man...
(remedial work
as per schedule)

the potter's hand
is the *primum mobile*
and my ancestry
is not in question.
Bad luck old sport.

See my father's face
my brother's shoulders
spun in clay
and water
out of the centrifuge.

V
In a Cave
    In a cave in Cornwall
    or possibly Devon
    they found a skull
    from the iron age

    and nearby they found
    his descendent
    still living in the same place
    a teacher

    which goes to show
    several things
    not the least of which is
    that travel broadens the mind.

VI
The Genome Project
    Neurons fire against the gloom
    dry lightning along the ridges
    and in the distant flats
    stripped by the tide
    a little light on the subject.

    God is in demand.
    Lo there is existence and faith
    although we have it arseways
    and death and glory
    and just enough useful code
    to make a little bastard
    mad enough to destroy us all
    and another to rip us off.

VII
Progress

    The scale is immense
    zero to infinity
    being as ephemeron
    a blinking eye.

    We come out of the sink
    and we die
    snowblind earthbound
    faulty.

    The computations
    terrify
    the profit and loss
    the currency

    the who begat whom
    and the why
    and the where have they gone
    without me.